EASTERN WISDOM

Priya Hemenway

EVERGREEN

EVERGREEN is an imprint of
TASCHEN GmbH

© 2007 TASCHEN GmbH
Hohenzollernring 53, D-50672 Köln
www.taschen.com

© 2006 by Book Laboratory Inc.

Lay out: Amy Ray

Production English edition: Textcase, Hilversum, Netherlands
Typesetting cover for Textcase:
Elixyz Desk Top Publishing, Groningen, Netherlands

Printed in Singapore

ISBN-13: 978-3-8228-1668-4
ISBN-10: 3-8228-1668-X

Contents

INTRODUCTION

The spiritual traditions of the East have fascinated Westerners for centuries and the wisdom that evolved in lands that are far away is as meaningful for us now as it has been for thousands of years. Eastern wisdom has grown out of the spiritual awakenings of men and women who devoted their lives to inner transformation and their words speak to the human need for inner peace.

The art that developed alongside the spiritual practices of the East is beautiful. Temples that reach into the sky have been the gathering places of the devout for centuries, lavishly illustrated manuscripts preserve ancient knowledge, and paintings on walls glorify the spirit of all those who have contributed to humankind's search to understand who and what we really are.

We all know that life is mysterious. We all search for answers. This has always been the case and always will be. This little book of Eastern wisdom tells the stories, and presents the truths that ancient seekers discovered. Beginning with Sufism in the Middle East and traveling via Taoism in China to Zen in Japan, it traces the development of three very different paths of wisdom, paths that evolved as men and women, seekers of truth, charted their experiences.

Each of these three traditions brings forth wisdom of a slightly different hue. Sufism, the most recent to evolve, was born out of Islam, a religion of devotion to a single God. Its wisdom lies within the human heart, and Sufis speak to us of the Beloved or Allah. The wisdom of the Sufis has two distinct voices—one speaking to us in poetry from love's great heights and the other speaking to us in parables and tales.

Tao, the ancient wisdom of China, found its clearest voice in Lao Tzu and his immortal *Tao Te Ching*, a short work that is based in centuries-long observation of the ways of the natural world. Lao Tzu, and those who follow him, practice a wisdom that is based on the eternally creative laws of nature.

Zen, one of the many flowerings of Buddhism, began with Gautama Buddha in India and was carried by a succession of great sages to Japan. Speaking to us through the voices of humor and pristine clarity, Zen is a wisdom which points to the truths that are experienced in the here and now.

The common thread that underlies all three wisdoms is the desire to untangle the mysteries of the soul. Understanding that we have somehow fallen asleep to our true nature, mystics and sages of Sufism, Tao, and Zen talk of awakening,

of becoming enlightened, of finding a treasure. Believing that there is more to life than meets the eye, they searched within and discovered universal truths regarding human existence. Having realized for themselves the eternal nature of the human soul, they have found ways to help others to experience its reality.

These great sages taught from their own unique experiences. Their wisdom, and the voices that echo in our hearts as we listen to their truths, are the voices that have inspired countless seekers to search within—where the treasure that is sought, lies buried.

SUFISM: WAY OF THE HEART

Sufism is known to many as the way of the heart, the path of the beloved. It is an inner wisdom that speaks in the language of love, and is a way of looking more deeply into ourselves through the eyes of God.

God, say Sufis, was a hidden treasure who wanted to be known, and so gave birth to the whole creation in order to be seen. It is God within ourselves that longs to meet the world, and only we ourselves who stand in the way.

Longing to be permanently held in the embrace of the Beloved (God), Sufis prepare by renouncing outer wealth, believing that the real treasure lies within. The word "Sufi" literally means "wearing wool" and refers to the simple clothes worn by early ascetics. In Islam, Sufis are those who follow the path of *tasawwuf*. Tasawwuf means "abandoning the world" and the people who follow the path of tasawwuf are mystics who live in the world but are not blinded by the world. They are on a journey to find God.

The journey that is undertaken by Sufis is undertaken by all those who seek to know themselves. It is a journey of self-discovery and it is universally understood that the goal of this journey cannot be reached through the intellect. A direct, or mystical, experience is needed.

The Greek root of the word mystical—*myein*—means "to close the eyes." This hints to the truth that is known to mystics everywhere that to experience God, or Truth, or any real aspect of ourselves, we must close our eyes and look within.

Looking within, Sufis search for God. Living in the marketplace of the world, they become so impassioned with their love that the world ceases to be a distraction and they see His reflection everywhere. They so abandon themselves to the love of God that they become His very eyes and ears. Through their complete surrender, Sufis become the very heartbeat of the Beloved.

Roots of Sufism

The roots of Sufism lie in the same Middle Eastern myths and events upon which Christianity and Judaism are also founded. Emerging out of the faith of Islam, Sufism appeared shortly after the death of the Prophet Muhammad. It is at the heart of this widespread religion, and is often referred to as the mystical aspect of Islam.

Islam in Arabic means "submission." It also means "surrender" and derives from a word meaning "peace," for, say Muslims, it is through surrendering our heart to God that we find fulfillment and peace in our lives. Islam's universal message of peace was announced to the Prophet Muhammad by the archangel Gabriel and is revealed to humanity in the Qur'an, the actual Word of God. The Qur'an is a book of lessons, a book of truth, and a book that teaches love and compassion.

The words of the Qur'an were spoken by Muhammad to his followers who wrote them down. During his lifetime the verses were ordered and twenty years after his death an official text was agreed upon and copies placed in every Muslim city. The Qur'an has remained unaltered for fourteen hundred years.

God is the Light
of the heavens and the earth.
The parable of His light
is as if there were a niche
and within it a lamp.
The lamp is enclosed in glass,
and shines like a brilliant star:
It is lit by the oil of the blessed olive tree
that comes neither from the East nor the West,
and the lamp is well nigh luminous
though fire has not touched it.
Light upon Light!
God guides those who follow Him
to His Light,
and speaking to all humanity
He speaks in parables
and is the fullness of all things.

(Q 24:35)

For thousands of years before the birth of Islam the Middle East had been a melting pot of different cultures. Nations came and went in successive waves of conquest, and people migrated from place to place. Many different roads met and made the Middle East a converging point for religion and philosophy as well as politics and trade.

At the dawn of the Christian era the Mediterranean world and most of the Near East was controlled by the imperial legions of Rome. Facing the eastern edge of the Roman Empire another strong power emerged—Persia. In the third century long and savage wars erupted between the two superpowers, during which Rome steadily lost territory to the Persians.

Meanwhile, the region of southern Arabia had seen the rise of a number of small city states with ancient tribal loyalties and a polytheistic culture. Neither the Romans nor the Persians had been able to annex these lands where civilization consisted mainly of a web of camel tracks and occasional settlements, with groups of insurgents roaming freely.

Into this arena fraught with political and religious wars, social discontent, and a yearning for something better, Muhammad brought the religion of Islam.

Muhammad

Muhammad was born in Mecca in 570 C.E.. Following a long line of earlier prophets including Abraham, Moses, John the Baptist, and Jesus Christ, Muhammad's mission was to rid southern Arabia of polytheism and to restore it to monotheism.

Quiet and thoughtful as a youth, Muhammad developed strong moral principles early in life. He became an honest and reliable trader and carried his wares to fairs where he came into contact with people from China, India, Persia, and the West, and where he was nicknamed "the honest one." He married a well-to-do widow named Khadijah, for whom he worked, and who admired his honest character. They fell deeply in love, and she became one of his strongest supporters.

Muhammad had always been interested in spiritual matters and developed the practice of retreating to isolated caves to meditate and pray for guidance. It was during one of these sojourns in the year 610 that he witnessed the first of a series of visitations from the angel Gabriel, informing him that he was to be blessed with the gift of prophecy and was to be the messenger of Allah.

Terrified, Muhammad pleaded that he was unable to do this. Gabriel repeated his command three times, and Muhammad, shaken by the experience and doubting his own senses, went home and told his wife Khadijah what had happened. Convinced of the reality of what had occurred and that the revelation was indeed divine, she reassured her husband.

The night of this first revelation is known as the Night of Power. Other revelations followed at regular intervals, and Muhammad began to speak fervently of them to his closest friends. "There is only one God," he repeated. "He is the same for all humanity, and all humanity must bow down before Him."

Three years after the initial revelation, Gabriel commanded Muhammad to preach openly, and so Muhammad began to make public attacks on polytheism. He gained new followers as news of his teachings spread. Leaders of local tribes became worried, for they feared for their own authority. Muhammad and his followers were persecuted by these local leaders. As opposition grew, life became increasingly difficult for his followers .

One night, Muhammad was awakened in the middle of the night by the archangel Gabriel and carried on a heavenly steed to Jerusalem where he met

with the spirits of Abraham, Moses, and Jesus, and together they all prayed. From Jerusalem Gabriel took Muhammad on a further journey through the seven heavens until finally Muhammad arrived at the Throne of God.

Shortly after he had this vision, Muhammad, fearing for his life, fled Mecca with his best friend, Abu Bakr. They spent the night in a cave, and while they slept a spider spun its web across the entrance. Spotting the unbroken web, the tribesmen who were looking for him rode on, and Muhammad was saved.

From this point on tribal loyalties were replaced by loyalty to the growing spiritual community of God—a community which, under the leadership of Muhammad, grew in strength and numbers. These changing loyalties united the people of numerous small tribes into the emerging nation of Islam.

In 632 Muhammad died after a short illness. Many followers refused to believe that he was dead until Abu Bakr stepped forward. Addressing the crowd that had gathered before Muhammad's house, he said "Whoever worshipped Muhammad, let him know that Muhammad is dead, but whoever worshipped God, let him know that God lives and dies not!"

Sufi Saints

In the years following the death of Muhammad, amongst the many who followed his teachings there were some whose hearts were set on fire by his message. They were the first Sufis. Not content to simply believe the truths the Prophet spoke concerning God, they devoted themselves to realizing them by experiencing God directly.

In the following pages you will meet Rabia al-Adawiyya and Mansur al-Hallaj, two of many, many Sufi saints who realized God.

Rabia is remembered fondly as the first true saint of Islam. The fact that she was a woman is only part of what makes her so remarkable. What truly touches all those who hear her story is her remarkable devotion and the wit with which she spread her teaching.

Mansur is remembered for his powerful phrase "*Ana al-haqq*"—"I am the Truth." Like Christ, Mansur is a martyr in the eyes of all those who read about the mystical traditions, for his words are spoken directly from the heart and tell a truth that few are brave enough to die for.

Rabia al-Adawiyya

Rabia al-Adawiyya was born near the town of Basra, Iraq in about 717 C.E. in the turbulent years of the first century after the death of the Prophet Muhammad.

Her father, Ismail, was a very poor and holy man who married and went to live with his wife on the edge of the desert. They had a daughter whom the father named Rabia. Then they had another daughter whom the father named Rabia ath-thani, and a third daughter he named Rabia ath-thalata, and then another daughter whom he named Rabia ar-rabia. This last child was to become the saint.

As the four girls grew up, their father Ismail worked hard to make a living for his family in the desert. He died when Rabia was eleven, and her mother, finding life in the desert too difficult for them, decided to take her four daughters to Basra where she hoped to make a better living. However, on their way they were set upon by bandits and the mother was killed. Each of the daughters was taken as a slave by one of the robbers.

Rabia's master took her to Baghdad where he set about using her to make money for himself. She was very beautiful and also had a lovely voice, so he taught her how to sing and dance and he sent her to weddings and celebrations where people would give her money which she passed on to him. Thus it was that Rabia developed many bad habits and lived a miserable life. But suddenly one day, when she was about thirty-six years old, she was singing at a wedding and to her surprise found herself singing in a different way.

Songs began to pour forth from her heart. They were addressed to her Beloved who was her true Love. Allah, the All-Mighty, had awakened in Rabia's heart.

> *I have made You the Companion of my heart.*
> *My body is available to those who desire its company,*
> *and is friendly toward all,*
> *but the Beloved of my heart is the guest of my soul.*

She immediately abandoned everything she had been doing and refused to sing or to dance or to play any music for anyone except for her Beloved Allah. This angered her master. He began to beat her and burn her, hoping that this would frighten her into returning to her former self.

But Rabia refused to respond to him. She began to pray all through the night, crying to Allah for help in her desperate state. Her master, seeing that he could not get her to change, and because he no longer had any use for her, decided to sell the young woman. Putting a cord around her neck, he dragged her to the slave market at Baghdad.

There a holy man bought Rabia and took her to his home, gave her food and clothes, and told her that he did not want anything from her, except that she should pray and be free in his house. Rabia thanked him with all her heart and said, "If you want anything from me that will serve Allah, He will give you your reward, but if you want anything from me for yourself only, I have nothing to give you."

The holy man replied that he would like to marry her and free her from being a slave, but that he would not ask it from her unless she wanted it. Rabia thanked him for his consideration and said that she did not want to marry anyone, but was grateful for the way that he cared for her.

"I exist only through Allah and I belong wholly to Him. You must ask for my hand from Him, and not from me."

There were many who heard of Rabia and came to visit her. She welcomed them and spoke to them from her heart. Many miracles are attributed to her, and apparently she was offered large sums for curing people. Once when she was offered a bag of gold she responded "If you leave that here, flies will gather as if a horse just relieved himself, and I might slip in it while dancing."

One day Hasan al-Basri saw her praying near a lake. Throwing his prayer rug on top of the water, he said, "Rabia come! Let us pray here."

She replied, "Hasan, when you are showing off your spiritual goods in the worldly market, you should do things which your fellows cannot do," and she threw her prayer rug into the air and climbed up onto it. "Come up here,

Hasan, where people can see us." Realizing that Hasan felt bad at being outsmarted, Rabia sought to console him. "Hasan, what you did, fishes can do, and what I did, flies can do. Our real business is not in performing tricks. We must both apply ourselves to the real business."

One day Rabia met a man and asked him how he was. He replied, "I have walked the path of obedience and I have not sinned since Allah created me."

She surprised him by speaking to his vanity, "Alas my friend, your existence is a sin to which no other sin can be compared."

Rabia's attraction to poverty grew out of her desire not to be distracted from her inner journey by the necessity of material considerations. A well-known story concerning this is told by one of her companions.

He had gone to visit Rabia in her house and saw she had nothing but a broken water pitcher out of which she drank, an old reed mat upon which she slept, and a brick which she used as a pillow. Seeing her impoverishment he felt sad and said to her, "I have many rich friends. If you wish I will get some household items from them for you."

She asked him, "Is not my provider and theirs one and the same?"

He answered, "Yes," to which she replied, "And has the provider of the poor forgotten them on account of their poverty? Does He prefer the rich because of their riches? Does He show them any greater love?"

"No."

"Then since He knows of my state, why should I remind Him? Such is His will and I wish only what He wills."

Rabia's love for her Beloved was passionate and all-consuming, but also full of humility and reverence. When she was asked how she came to live in such a state she replied "Everything I had lost in life, I found in Him."

As she neared the end of her life, Rabia moved to Jerusalem where she lived in a small house on the Mountain of Olives. She taught at a local temple and after her death a tomb, which still exists, was built by her followers. Rabia is fondly remembered, by all who hear tales told of her, for her unconditional love.

Mansur al-Hallaj

Mansur al-Hallaj was one the most controversial of all Sufi saints. He became a complete embodiment of oneness with Allah and his life is a pinnacle in Islamic history. Sufism was new at the time he lived, and Mansur provoked extensive opposition from the orthodoxy. Even his own Sufi master, Junaid, considered his public behavior undisciplined and dangerous. He was finally crucified in 922 and is remembered for his famous cry "Ana al-haqq"—"I am the Truth." This is his story.

Mansur was born in a village in southern Persia, in 857. He was the son of a cotton merchant and as a young child was drawn towards a spiritual life. At the age of sixteen he memorized the Qur'an and at eighteen he left home and went to Baghdad where Junayd accepted him and became his Master.

The young man was seized by a strong desire to dissolve into God. Like a river flowing from its source to the ocean, nothing could stop his course.

Having spent a short time in Baghdad with Junayd, Mansur went on a pilgrimage to Mecca. He was away for a year in which he gave himself difficult spiritual tasks to fulfill. When he returned to Baghdad he went to see his Master. Hearing a knock on the door, Junayd asked, "Who is there?" Mansur responded with his famous reply, "Ana al-haqq"—I am the Truth."

Junayd, realizing that what he said was true, but knowing how easily it could be misunderstood, cautioned him sternly, "Be careful about the Secret of Love. Do not speak it to those who cannot understand." Then he added, "The time will soon come when you will burn like a piece of wood."

Mansur replied with sorrow, "The day I burn as a piece of wood, you will be wearing the clothes of the orthodoxy."

He then began to roam about Baghdad, and everywhere he went people gathered to listen to him. They drank from his words, for he spoke to them of the secrets that lie in their own hearts. They called him al-Hallaj of the Secrets.

Orthodox Muslims took exception to the crazed utterances of Mansur and grew angry with him. They could not understand how anyone could utter such things as he did, and one by one, even the Sufis began to turn against him and to shun his company.

Mansur longed only to live in the constant state of overflowing love in which there were no restrictions. He returned time and time again to his ecstatic states and compared himself to a moth that is attracted to the flame of a candle, slowly approaching it until it is burned. He said that he, like the moth, wanted only to throw himself into the flame—to throw himself into the Fire of Love—and to be consumed by it.

One of his young followers, Ibrahim ibn Fatik, went to see Mansur at his home one day. When he arrived he saw his Master standing on his head.

Sensing the presence of Ibrahim, Mansur told him to come in and not be afraid. So Ibrahim went in and sat down before Mansur, whose eyes were like two burning flames. "Some people call me an unbeliever, and others call me a saint. Those who call me an unbeliever and turn against me are dearer to me."

Ibrahim asked him why and Mansur replied, "Those who call me a saint do so from some good opinion they have of me, while those who call me an unbeliever do so from zealous defense of their own convictions. He who defends what he believes is dearer to Allah than he who simply carries good opinions."

When he talked like this, people were confused and thought him dangerous. They told him it would be better if he hid his thoughts and did not make such a show of his experiences.

Mansur made a second pilgrimage to Mecca, but when he arrived he was denounced as a heretic and a magician so he took a boat to India and from there he traveled to China. He met many people on his travels and spoke to thousands. He sowed the seeds of a great and impassioned love for God, and it is said that the phrases he uttered can still be found in the poetry of the regions he visited. When he again returned to Baghdad many of his foreign friends wrote him letters, which made those in the government suspicious. They began to look upon him as a threat to their security and the stability of their power.

Attacks mounted against him and Mansur was eventually thrown into prison where he spent eleven years and where he was finally brutally tortured and crucified. There were many witnesses who said that at the end he was strangely serene and that he forgave his persecutors. He is referred to as the martyr of mystical love.

I am He Whom I love, and He Whom I love is I.
We are two spirits dwelling in one body.
If you see me, you see Him;
And if you see Him, you see us both.

I saw my Lord with the Eye of my heart,
And I said: Truly there is no doubt that it is You.
It is You that I see in everything;
And I do not see You through anything but You.

I wonder at You and me.
You annihilated me out of myself into You.
You made me near to Yourself,
So that I thought that I was You,
And You were me."

MANSUR AL-HALLAJ

112 Mowlana Djelaleddin, a turk of Natoly,
author of the Mesnevi Romi, an excellent lit treatise
of Ethics in Persian verses, sung all over Persia, turky
and in India in Companiese.

Sufi Poetry

Sufis are recognized for their beautiful love poems in which words of wisdom are lodged in the language of love. Most well known are the exquisite poems of Jalaluddin Rumi, but there are many others whose language explores the subtle regions of the heart.

The following poem was written by Farid ud Din Attar who lived in the twelfth century in a town called Nishapur in northeastern Iran. It is said that as a youth, he worked in his father's pharmacy where he prepared drugs and attended patients. Upon his father's death, he became the owner of his own store.

Work in the pharmacy was difficult for Attar as people from all walks of life visited the shop and shared their troubles with him. One day, an old man walked in and the way he looked at the wares of the store made Attar uneasy. He ordered the man to leave.

Looking the owner and the well-stocked shop over, the man said, "I have no difficulty going anywhere. All I have is this ragged coat on my back. But you, how can you, with all this," waving his arm around the room, "plan to leave!"

This response affected Attar deeply. He thought about it for many days, and eventually decided to give up his shop and seek a teacher.

After many years Attar returned to Nishapur where he settled, reopened the pharmacy, and began to write poetry.

The whole world is a marketplace for Love,
For naught that is, from Love remains remote.
The Eternal Wisdom made all things in Love.
On Love they all depend, to Love all turn.
The earth, the heavens, the sun, the moon, the stars
The center of their orbit find in Love.
By Love are all bewildered, stupefied,
Intoxicated by the Wine of Love.

From each, Love demands a mystic silence.
What do all seek so earnestly? 'Tis Love.
Love is the subject of their inmost thoughts,
In Love no longer "Thou" and "I" exist,
For self has passed away in the Beloved.
Now will I draw aside the veil from Love,
And in the temple of mine inmost soul
Behold the Friend, Incomparable Love.
He who would know the secret of both worlds
Will find that the secret of them both is Love.

FARID UD DIN ATTAR

Sufi Tales

The wisdom of the Sufis has been passed on for generations through their tales, famous for their wonderful humor and mystical meanings. Most well known are the stories about Mullah Nasruddin, a colorful character whose practical wisdom is displayed through his very enlightening encounters.

One day Mullah Nasruddin lost his ring down in the basement of his house, where it was very dark. There being no chance of his finding it in that darkness, he went out on the street and started looking for it there. A passerby stopped and inquired:

"What are you looking for, Mullah Nasruddin? Have you lost something?"

"Yes, I've lost my ring down in the basement."

"But Mullah Nasruddin, why don't you look for it down in the basement where you have lost it?" asked the man in surprise.

"Don't be silly, man! How do you expect me to find anything in that darkness!"

Mullah Nasruddin was dreaming one night that someone had counted nine gold pieces into his hand and he was insisting that he would not accept less than ten. While he was arguing with the man over the one gold piece, he was awakened by a sudden noise in the street.

Seeing that his hand was empty, Mullah Nasruddin quickly closed his eyes, extended his hand as if he was ready to receive, and said, "Very well, my friend, have it your way. Give me nine."

Once a famous philosopher was traveling through Nasruddin's village. He invited Nasruddin to join him for dinner. Nasruddin accompanied him to a local restaurant, where they asked the waiter about the special of the day.

"Fish! Fresh Fish!" replied the waiter.

"Bring us two," they answered.

A few minutes later, the waiter brought out a large platter with two cooked fish on it, one of which was quite a bit smaller than the other. Nasruddin took the larger of the fish and placed in on his plate. The philosopher, giving Nasruddin a look of intense disbelief, proceed to tell him that what he did was not only blatantly selfish, but that it violated the principles of almost every known moral and ethical system. Nasruddin listened to the man patiently. When he finished, Nasruddin said, "Well, Sir, what would you have done?"

"I, being a conscientious human, would have taken the smaller fish for myself."

"And here you are," Nasruddin said, and placed the smaller fish on the gentleman's plate.

Equally well known in the Muslim world are the many stories that have been told by Sufi masters to instruct their disciples. One of the most beautiful is the Tale of the Sands which talks of the voice that whispers its secrets to us all.

A stream, tumbling down from its source in the mountains was suddenly brought to a halt when it reached the desert. Having crossed every other barrier the stream was convinced that it would not be hard to cross the sands and tried, yet could find no way.

A wind came up and the sands whispered to the stream, "The wind crosses the desert...."

The stream was perplexed. "The wind can fly. Of course it can cross the desert."

The voice continued, "Dashing yourself upon the sands will drain you. You will disappear if you do not allow the wind to carry you."

"Carry me?" thought the stream. "How can the wind carry me?"

The voice of the sands insisted, "The wind performs this function all the time. It lifts the water up, carries it across the desert, and then drops it down on the other side."

"How can this be?" asked the river in disbelief.

"It is simply so. If you don't do it, you will be left here and you will disappear into the sands."

"But if I listen to you, I don't know what will happen. There is no guarantee that what you are telling me is true."

"True," said the voice. "In either case you will cease to be the same stream you are today. Your problem stems from the fact that you are unaware of your essential nature. If you knew that, you would happily rise up into the arms of the wind."

As he heard this, a vague memory stirred in the mind of the stream. He had a strange sensation that he had once before been held in the arms of the wind. Suddenly, impulsively, he raised his arms.

He turned into vapor and was carried many, many miles across the desert. Finally reaching a mountain range at the far side of the desert, the stream began to turn to rain and fell to the ground.

Because of his doubts, the stream was able to record in his mind the details of the journey and as he fell into the sea he reflected that he had now found his essential nature. He had learned much.

The sands meanwhile, acknowledged amongst themselves how they see this same thing happen every day, and thus it is said that the way in which the Stream of Life continues on its journey is written in the sands.

So it is with stories of their saints, poetry, and tales of mystery that Sufis are instructed in the subtle ways of the human heart. The lessons they learn are of trust, humility, and love. The enigmatic wisdom of the Sufis is sometimes hard to grasp, but like the Beloved, grows clearer, richer, and more beautiful as its many facets are discovered. The wisdom of the Sufis begins with the heart. The heart is a door to ecstasy and it is in ecstasy that we find the keys to the eternal kingdom of life.

TAO: HARMONY WITH NATURE

Tao is a wisdom of harmony. Its founder, Lao Tzu, author of the famous *Tao Te Ching*, was a man who reflected upon the natural world and drew from nature the truths that make Taosim unique. He noticed that chaos results in a delicate balance that supports the weak as well as the strong; and that taking a path of least resistance is the way that rivers run. He wove these and other principles into a short doctrine of eighty-one verses which has been read time and time again by those who seek peace and self-realization.

The *Tao Te Ching* was originally written on slats of bamboo, twenty-five hundred years ago. Not only does it form the basis of Taoism, it is the basis for the Chinese system of health that is renowned for its beneficial effects. The *Tao Te Ching* was followed by two other works, the *Chuang Tzu* and the *Leih Tzu*, which were written by Lao Tzu's disciples. Together these three books are considered to be the classics of Taoism.

History of Taoism

The roots of Taoism reach far back into prehistory to a time when the people of China lived in accordance with natural laws. Looking at the footprints of birds in the snow they developed a system of writing, and watching the patterns of nature they evolved a cosmology that made practical sense. Heaven and earth were not separate for these early people, and humanity and nature were not divided.

The Shang dynasty (c. 1500–1100 B.C.E.) is the earliest period in China for which historical records exist. We know that at this time it fell to the male head of the family to carry out its religious rituals. As the family grew into a tribe, and the tribe into a nation, the model was retained. Government was not separate from religion and there was no priestly caste. The emperors who ruled the country performed its sacred rites and on their shoulders rested responsibility for all that happened in their lands.

A story comes to us from these early times that tells of a the flooding of the legendary River Lo. It was apparent to the emperor of the land that in order for the flood waters to recede, a sacrifice was needed, but each time one was

made, a turtle emerged from the river, circled the sacrifice, and returned to the water. The flood would not abate.

Trying to figure out what to do, the emperor was standing on the edge of the river one day, deep in contemplation. Looking down, he saw that a turtle had emerged and was circling his feet. Carefully observing its back, he noticed very pronounced markings that looked like numbers. Adding up these numbers in many different ways, the emperor arrived each time with the number fifteen. He applied these markings to the sacrifice and the flood waters abated rewarding the emperor and his people with prosperity.

The magical markings on the turtle's back are believed to have led to the development of the theory of yin-yang and the eight trigrams which contain the secrets of all the various cycles of life. Yin and yang are the two opposing energies that are the manifestations of Heaven and Earth and which, through their fluctuation and interaction give rise to the five elements and the ten thousand things.

The five elements are water, fire, wood, metal, and earth. Besides being the elements that determine all natural phenomena, they also represent the five phases of transformation. It lies in the nature of water to moisten and to flow downward; of fire to heat and to rise; of wood to bend and straighten again; of metal to be cast or hammered into various forms; and of earth to be fertile.

"The ten thousand things" is an expression that describes absolutely everything in our universe—real, abstract, energetic, and symbolic.

For the early people of China, the abstract world of the spirit was very real. They believed that the human soul consists of two parts: One is earthly by nature, while the other is heavenly. After death the earthly part (*kuie*) lingers for a while near the body it inhabited and then is absorbed back into the earth from whence it re-emerges as more life. The other part (*shen*) rises into the heavens where it functions as part of the spirit world of the ancestors—a world for which the Chinese have enormous respect. The "spirit of the ancestors" is the force that ensures fertility in a family and protects it from harm.

The early Chinese concept of god is an extension of the spirit of the ancestors and the human souls they emerge from. Their gods are outstanding human beings, such as emperors or great sages, who have been elevated to function in the more abstract realms after their death. Thus the people of the Chinese

empire have a celestial administration which mirrors its earthly one.

Along with the spirit world of the ancestors that protects them, they recognize another energy, called Te, which is the nature, good or bad, that each human is born with. Te is the quality that makes great men great and enables an emperor to overcome his enemies, win the support of the people, and achieve influence and authority.

The Age of One Hundred Philosophers

Around the year 1100 B.C.E. the ancient Shang government was overthrown by tribes of barbarians from the fringes of the empire. The old government had become morally corrupt and could not withstand the invasion. The new rulers, called Chou, ruled until 770 B.C.E. when they in turn become corrupt and were forced out by a new group of barbaric invaders. The peasants of China began to rebel and make war—not against the barbarians who pressed at the outer borders of their kingdom, but against their own rulers.

War led to more war, treachery to more treachery, and it seemed that China was being reduced to a wasteland. It was at this time that Lao Tzu, as well as hundreds of other thinkers, philosophers, and mystics roamed the country with their disciples, teaching the citizenry and trying to convince the rulers to put new philosophical ideas into practice. This period is sometimes referred to as the Age of One Hundred Philosophers, with each philosopher putting forth a vision of what the new social order of the country ought to be and expounding on human nature and the nature of existence.

Confucius (551–479 B.C.E.) believed that the only way a political system could be made to work properly was for each person to act according to prescribed relationships. "Let the ruler be a ruler and the subject a subject," he said, but added that to rule properly a ruler must be virtuous.

Mencius (372–289 B.C.E.), a disciple of Confucius, declared that man was by nature good and that people should be governed by those they approved of, while Xun Zi (300–237 B.C.E.) preached that man is innately evil and that the best government is based on authoritarian control.

Li Si (d. 208 B.C.E.) maintained that human nature is incorrigibly selfish, and therefore the only way to preserve the social order is to impose strict discipline.

Mo Zi (470–391 B.C.E.) said that all men are created equal and that mankind should follow heaven by practicing universal love.

Lao Tzu

It was into this period of political upheaval and social unrest that Lao Tzu appeared. The Taoist sage proposed that the best way cope with the tyranny of government was to do nothing at all. To suggest such a theory of inaction in times of unrest would perhaps seem irresponsible, but with Nature as a model, it is absolutely viable.

There are some scholars who deny that someone named Lao Tzu existed. Legend however, tells us that the story of his life began one day at the end of summer when an extraordinary event took place. A woman leaned up against a plum tree and gave birth to a child. Having given birth, the woman died, leaving the child alone in the world, but the infant was quite clever and able to speak as soon as he was born. Pointing to the plum tree his mother had leaned against at his birth, he announced that he wanted to take his family name from the tree that had supported her. To the word "plum" (*li*) he added the word "ear" (*erh*), because he had been born with very large ears, and so he became Li Erh. However, because his hair was already snow white, most people called him Lao Tzu, or "Old Man."

Nothing is known of Lao Tzu's youth. He spent his adult years in the imperial capital, first as palace secretary and then as keeper of the calendar for the court. In this position he would have read from religious texts and might have had some political influence. He was respected as a teacher and a sage, for the "tzu" that was attached to his name indicates he was a man of wisdom.

There is a story in a later book of history that tells of a meeting between Lao Tzu and the philosopher Confucius. Confucius, in the manner of someone who thinks himself to be superior, asked Lao Tzu what he thought about the great teachers of the past.

"The bones of those of whom you speak have long since turned to dust; only their words have been preserved for us."

"In any case, if time and fortune favor a person, he travels to court in a carriage. If they do not favor him, he roams about as a beggar."

"I have heard it said that a good merchant will conceal his wealth and act as if he were poor, and a noble person with sufficient inner virtue will likely give the appearance of a fool. Therefore, O Pretentious One! give up your high-

handed manner, your desires, your vanity, and your pretentious zeal—for they are no use to you."

Confucius went home and told his followers:

"I know that a bird can fly, a fish can swim, and an animal can run. To catch that which runs, a trap can be set; for that which swims, a net can be thrown; for that which flies, an arrow can be shot. But how to catch a dragon ascending into heaven on the wind and the clouds is beyond my knowledge. Today I have seen Lao Tzu, and he is like that dragon."

After a long and healthy life, Lao Tzu, at the age of 160, decided to retreat into the mountains to end his days. Sitting on the back of a water buffalo, he left his friends behind and rode away. When he arrived at the Han-ku Pass, which leads westward toward Tibet, he was met by the keeper of the pass, a man named Yin Hsi, who had just woken from a dream in which Lao Tzu had appeared. He was saddened when he heard that the Old Man was leaving, for along with many of his countrymen, Yin Hsi loved and respected Lao Tzu and was sorry to see him passing away. He asked Lao Tzu to stop for a short while at the top of the mountain and to record the essence of his teaching so that Yin Hsi and other followers would have something to refer to when they forgot the Way.

Lao Tzu agreed, and went off for three days. He returned with a slim volume composed of five thousand characters. Having completed the book, Lao Tzu departed for the West. We do not know when or where he died.

The Tao Te Ching

The small book that Lao Tzu wrote was originally called the *Lao Tzu* after its author. It was assiduously studied by Chinese nobility in the Imperial Academy during the Tang Dynasty (618–907 C.E.) and the word Ching, or "sacred book," was attached to the words Tao and Te, and the *Lao Tzu* became the *Tao Te Ching*.

Although there are scholars who deny that Lao Tzu wrote the *Tao Te Ching* or that such a person even existed, these people cannot properly account for the origins of the book. They say that perhaps it was written by several people, one of whom was a historical person named Li Erh, or that it may have been written by a group of Taoist students or by thinkers who were sympathetic to the ways of Taoism. Regardless of how it was written, or by whom, the *Tao Te Ching* is the most important classic of Taoism and in spirit it honors all the enlightened masters of Eastern wisdom, for its truths are eternal and it has inspired countless seekers to pursue a path to awakening.

Tao, according to Lao Tzu, is the origin of everything. It is from Tao and toward Tao that all life moves. At the beginning and at the end there is Tao. By its nature it is indefinable; it is an emptiness, nothingness. It is perfectly still even while being in motion. To contemplate Tao is to contemplate the great mystery of life; to experience Tao is to have an experience which the mind cannot comprehend. To know Tao is to experience that which is eternal.

That which we sometimes call nature is also Tao. It is the energy of everything that grows, the very energy of life continually replenishing and decaying in its eternal, cyclical movement. Tao is the creative process by which male and female procreate. It can be seen in stars, heard in thunder, felt in chilly water. Tao is that which cannot be exhausted: The more it is drawn upon, the more it flows. Tao is the eternal energy creating and nourishing all things. We are not separate from it.

Te is the state of being through which Tao can move. It is uninhibited, innocent—the same quality that Lao Tzu attributes to a small child—and Tao flows freely through Te. Te is like the hollow reed through which the wind blows.

Te arises out of harmony and must be practiced; it does not arise on its own. Just as the musician practices and practices, and then lets go completely as the music rushes through, so the person seeking to embody Tao practices Te.

*The Tao that can be spoken
Is not the true Tao.
Any name which can be given to it
Is not its true name.*

*Tao cannot be seen; Tao cannot be heard;
Tao cannot be known in any way.
For Tao is hidden, and has no name.
Everything moves in Tao.*

*That which was before
Heaven and Earth is Tao.
Tao is the mother of all things.*

*Being of Tao, one endures forever;
Though the body perishes, one suffers not.*

*When Nature is about to withhold a thing
It is first sure to increase it.
When about to weaken,
It is first sure to strengthen.
When about to debase
it is certain first to exalt.*

When about to deprive,
it is first sure to give.
This is what I call the covert agreement.
The soft and the weak
easily overcome
the hard and the strong.

The greatest virtue is like water;
it is good to all things.
It attains the most inaccessible places
without effort.
Therefore it is like Tao,
which has the virtue of adapting itself.

Like the heart, it is virtuous by being deep.
Like speech, it is virtuous when it is quiet.
Like choice, it is virtuous in equanimity.
Like a servant, it is trustworthy.
It flows quickly sometimes,
and at others it trickles.
Like action it has its seasons.
And because it does not strive
it has no enemies.

Lao Tzu proposed that the best way to come to terms with the pillage, tyranny, slaughter, and war-hunger of the lords of his time was to do nothing at all. His theory of inaction—Wu Wei—was found in nature. Watching carefully he noted that every action will produce a reaction, every challenge will produce a response. If a wasp is being crushed it will sting. If an animal is cornered it will fight. Leaving things alone is Wu Wei.

Lao Tzu taught that nothing is achieved by being aggressive; to yield is to be preserved. Wu Wei is effortless. There is no obstacle and there is no fight.

Wu Wei is not idle inertia. It is a flow of energies that is constantly moving and always changing—but is utterly relaxed, making no effort.

A hurricane will not outlast the morning,
a heavy rain will not outlast the day.
Who has the power to hurry things?
If Heaven and Earth do not hurry them,
what shall a person do?

To express your courage outwardly
is to concern yourself with death.
To express your courage inwardly
is to encounter life.

———

There are two kinds of action:
One is outer and the other is inner.
But who is to say if one of them is better?
The Sage cannot tell.

———

The celestial Tao does not push,
yet it overcomes everything.
It does not speak, yet it acknowledges all.
It does not provoke, yet it cooperates.
It is quiet in its methods, yet always effective.

The wise are yielding,
like snow beneath the sun;
naked, like newly felled timber;
hollow, like the valley;
obscure, like muddy water.

May not one take muddy water
and make it clear by keeping still?

———

Both Heaven and Earth endure forever.
The cause of their endurance
is their indifference.

———

The net of Tao is wide,
and no one knows how it is cast.

Chuang Tzu

If little is known about Lao Tzu, even less is known about his disciples Chuang Tzu and Lieh Tzu. Both have authored books that bear their names and which are full of stories and sayings that are more down to earth than the *Tao Te Ching*.

Apart from the fact that Chuang Tzu was married, we only know that for a while he held a minor administrative post and that, being unwilling to serve under a prince or ruler, he resigned and moved to humble circumstances where he lived with his disciples and wrote the *Chunag Tzu*.

The most famous of all stories about him tells of the morning he awoke from a dream in which he was a butterfly. He looked so upset that one of his disciples asked him what was the matter.

"I am puzzled," said Chuang Tzu, "by a profound uncertainty. I do not know whether I am Chuang Tzu who last night dreamed he was a butterfly or whether I am a butterfly dreaming he is Chuang Tzu.

A historical work dating from a much later time tells another story about Chuang Tzu that emphasizes his very independent nature.

King Wen of Chou, having heard about Chuang Tzu's talents, sent a messenger laden with expensive presents and an invitation for the sage to join the court and offering him a post as minister.

Chuang Tzu laughed at the offer and said, "A thousand pieces of gold is no mean sum and the offer from the court is no doubt an honorable one; but have you ever seen an ox on its way to be slaughtered? Having been carefully fattened over a number of years, it is bedecked with colored ribbons and led to a great temple with much fanfare and fuss, but in that moment the ox would obviously prefer to be a cat or a dog. The trapppings are meaningless."

"Go away!" he said to the messenger. "Don't bother me! I would rather wallow joyfully in a dirty puddle than be led on a rope by the ruler of a kingdom. I live as I please and shall never accept an official post."

The book called *Chuang Tzu* consists of thirty-three chapters. The first seven are called the "inner" books and were actually written by Chuang Tzu. The other chapters are believed to be the work of his disciples. With tales, pieces of prose and bits of poetry, Chuang Tzu develops an argument for simplicity.

The point of a fish trap is to catch a fish: once you've got the fish, you can forget the trap. The point of a rabbit snare is to snare the rabbit: once you've got the rabbit, you can forget the snare. And the point of a word is to express an idea: once you've got the idea, you can forget the word. How can I find someone who's forgotten words, so we can have a few words together?

Great understanding is broad and unhurried;
Small understanding is cramped and busy.

Great words are bright and open;
Small words are chit and chat.

Great fear is wide open and calm;
Small fear is fever and worry.

If a man is crossing a river
and an empty boat collides with his own skiff,
even though he be a bad-tempered man
he will not become very angry.
But if he sees a man in the boat,
he will shout to him to steer clear.
And if the shout is not heard he will shout
again and yet again, and begin cursing…
and all because there is somebody in that boat.
Yet if the boat were empty, he would not be shouting
and he would not be angry.

If you can empty your own boat
crossing the river of the world,
no one will oppose you,
no one will seek to harm you.

Leih Tzu

Not much is known about Lieh Tzu except what he recounts about his own experiences as a disciple. One famous tale describes a lesson in humility.

Lieh Tzu, pretending he knew more than he did, gave an exhibition of his skill in archery to Po Hun. Placing a cup of water on his elbow, he shot his arrows.

"Bravo!" said Po Hun, "that is really excellent, but your stance is not like that of one who is above passion. Come with me." They went to the edge of a cliff which Po Hun approached by walking backwards until his feet overhung the edge. He beckoned to Lieh Tzu to approach the edge, but Lieh Tzu was lying prostrate on the ground, covered with sweat.

Po Hun said "The perfect man soars to the blue sky above, or dives down to the yellow springs below, or traverses the eight ends of the great compass, without a change in countenance or unevenness in breathing. You are terrified. Your internal economy is defective. You have no Tao."

With this, Lieh Tzu went home to practice.

The *Book of Lieh Tzu* is full of practical anecdotes and sayings. Although obscure in parts, it does not contain the infinite possibilities of misunder-standing common to the *Tao Te Ching*.

If you do not know how to keep still in this crazy world, you will be drawn into all kinds of unnecessary trouble. You will lose your view of the Way, and, when you realize it, it will be too late, for in losing the Way, you have also lost yourself.

———

You can say that I started my learning with what was given to me at birth, continued with what was natural for me to do, and completed it by trusting what was meant to be.

———

If you don't have enough to eat, work on getting enough to eat.
If you can't keep warm in winter, work on getting sufficient clothing.
If you don't have time to enjoy yourself, work toward getting leisure time.
But when you have enough, you should stop.

Taoist Art

The art of Taoist landscape painting is inspired by the same deep communion with nature that gives rise to all Taoist wisdom. Before beginning to work, a Taoist painter immerses himself in what he is about to paint. If it is a bamboo grove, he might sit with the bamboo for half a day before making a stroke. Just like the musician who waits for the music to move through him, the Taoist painter waits for the brush to move.

Human beings are portrayed as being in harmony with their surroundings. Their part in the vastness of existence is very small and we have to look closely to find them in the paintings. Those we do see are usually carrying bundles, riding buffalo, or poling boats—signs that they are on a journey.

Permeating everything is a deep love and respect for the natural world. This love is the essence of Taoist wisdom. It is a tribute to the spirit of Lao Tzu and his disciples that the thoughts he expressed in the *Tao Te Ching* have inspired such beautiful art. The wisdom of Tao is perennial. Like nature, it never tires, and like nature, it is very immediate.

ZEN: THE EMPTY MIND

Westerners think of Zen as an approach to life that is simple and uncomplicated. It is an elegant practice of awareness that is based on techniques of meditation that encourage total relaxation and presence in the here and now.

Zen is an approach to living that is very easy to appreciate, less simple to grasp, and exceedingly difficult to practice, for Zen is about experiencing the present moment with an empty mind. This empty mind is not an irresponsible mind, nor is it a vacant or a hollow mind; it is a mind that has relinquished the need to conceptualize and has thus become free to respond spontaneously. With an empty mind, the practitioner of Zen experiences the richness of life one moment at a time without any fear of the past or concern about the future.

Birth of Zen

Zen was born out of a meeting of Buddhism and Taoism that happened in China at the end of the fifth century C.E. Called Ch'an in China, Zen ripened over many hundreds of years and was finally carried to Japan in the twelfth century. There it flourished. To understand Zen it is helpful to look at its roots in Buddhism.

Buddhism arose in India in the fifth century B.C.E. at about the same time that Taosim arose in China. It is based on the teachings of Gautama Buddha, who lived at a time when the ancient spiritual traditions of the land had become consolidated in the hands of priests who used religion as a way to enforce their own power. Gautama was a revolutionary. He took religion out of their hands and gave it back to humanity. He roamed around the country preaching that individuals are responsible for their own spiritual awakening.

Buddha himself was later denounced by the priests of Hinduism, and in the years following his death, his followers were forced to flee India. Thus Buddhism was carried to other parts of the Far East where it evolved into a variety of different forms, among them—Zen.

The Teachings of Gautama Buddha

The teachings of Buddha are fundamental to an understanding of Zen. Many of these teachings were formulated thousands of years before his birth by the ancient sages of Hinduism. Concepts such as reincarnation (which describes the process by which the human soul is reborn) and karma (the universal law of cause and effect by which goodness reaps happiness and evil reaps anguish) are the basis for a religiousness that is both compassionate and peaceful. Those who practice self-awareness and strive to engender no bad karma will be rewarded by greater peace. Those who forget these principles will live in greater misery.

These concepts gave rise to the two most basic teachings of Buddha. The first is called The Four Noble Truths, the second is called The Eightfold Way. These two teachings guide all Buddhists.

The story of Buddha's life tells that that as a young prince he was fervently protected by his father, who did not want to loose him to a path of spirituality. It had been forseen by astrologers that Gautama was to become either a great king and leader of men or a great mystic.

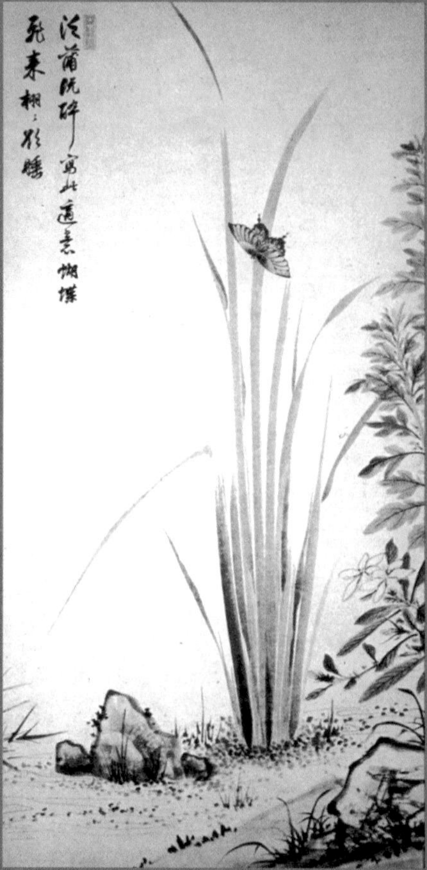

One day Gautama escaped the palace grounds and went into the local town where he was surprised to see that death and suffering are all around. He was profoundly moved and decided to go in search of that which does not die.

For many years he searched for an experience that would satisfy him and only when he had become perfectly awakened did he realize the keys. He set forth a teaching for all those who long to know themselves and he called this the Teaching of the Four Noble Truths. These four truths describe the essence of Buddhism.

The Four Noble Truths:

1) Suffering exists.
2) The cause of our suffering is unawareness.
3) The remedy for unawareness is meditation.
4) The practice of meditation is "right living."

Techniques of meditation had been taught by Hindu sages in India for centuries. What Buddha added to these techniques is in the practice of "right living."

The Eightfold Way of Right Living is a guide for those who wish to free themselves from the endless cycles of rebirth into lives of misery and suffering. These principles can be practiced by anyone at any time and keeping them in mind supports the meditations that ultimately lead to awakening. With the practice of the Eightfold Way, men and women became freed from the unnecessary constraints that were placed upon them by Hindu priests.

The Eightfold Way of Right Living:

1) Right Understanding: learning the laws of karma.
2) Right Thought: fostering thoughts of compassion.
3) Right Speech: speaking truth rather than lies.
4) Right Conduct: behaving in ways that are helpful.
5) Right Livelihood: earning a living in ways that promote happiness.
6) Right Effort: cultivating healthy states of mind.
7) Right Mindfulness: becoming more aware of thoughts and actions.
8) Right Meditation: deepening the practice of being present.

The teachings of Hinduism that gave rise to those of Gautama Buddha have been passed on for thousands of years. The fundamental purpose for which these teachings exist is to enlighten the people of the world; and those who have attained enlightenment are those who have found freedom from the unending cycles of birth and death through dissolving into *nirvana*, or the true and eternal nature of things.

Those who become awakened have always turned around to speak to those who yearn for their own enlightenment, and with this the tradition of masters and disciples evolved. The enlightened masters continue to pass on new techniques and truths that will help young disciples discover their own freedom in each new age.

Those who have become awakened are no longer slaves to desire, hatred, and delusion—the qualities that bind us to our misery. Enlightened, they live in this world, but are free of its draw. They have journeyed within and discovered the bliss of non-attachment and through the practice of meditation have learned to stay present to the here and now.

Gautama Buddha became enlightened at the age of thirty-five. Having attained a state of absolute awareness in which all desires ceased, he sat for some time in the ecstasy of silent blissfulness.

At first, he was unable to communicate what had happened, for enlightenment is an experience beyond words. A few companions with whom he had spent many years seeking, realized that something wonderful had happened to Gautama and they begged him to talk with them in any way he could.

With this Gautama Buddha became one of the world's most beloved teachers of wisdom. He moved around India for forty-five years and touched the lives of thousands, creating a *sangham* (community) of disciples and leading many towards their own enlightenment.

He made it a practice for the community to remain no longer than three days in any particular spot, for they depended on the generosity of others for food and shelter and he did not want to be a burden. At every village or town that he entered, Gautama would gather around himself all those who wished to hear his sermons, and it was with the deepest reverence that they listened to him speak.

Mahakashyapa

It was at one such gathering that Gautama Buddha appeared one day with a flower in his hand. The deep hush that usually announced his arrival grew deeper, for on this day, Gautama Buddha did not begin to talk. He simply sat in silence with the flower in his hand.

As the silence grew more difficult for many, it grew more profound for others. Finally, from the back of the gathering a loud and heartfelt laugh rang out. Buddha looked over to where the laugh had come from and as his eyes caught those of Mahakashyapa he smiled. Rising up from his seat, Gautama walked over to the laughing monk and handed him the flower, saying "What can be said, I have already said. What cannot be said, has been conveyed to Mahakashyapa."

With this Mahakashyapa became the first in a long line of disciples who were to receive a direct transmission from their masters—an experience that is called the "special transmission from heart-mind to heart-mind." This special transmission that was passed directly from Gautama Buddha to Mahakashyapa, and from Mahakashyapa to his own disciple, and so on for hundreds of years, is the special transmission of Zen. There were many other disciples of Buddha who attained enlightenment and who went on to teach, transform and enlighten people in other ways and Buddhism spread in a variety of forms into many countries. What happened to Mahakashyapa was special, though, because in an unbroken chain the experience was passed on through generations and generations of Buddhist masters and disciples until about 530 C.E., when a monk named Bodhidharma (the twenty-eighth in this line) fled persecution in India and went to China.

There were at this time thousands of Buddhist monks in China. Within a few hundred years after the death of Gautama Buddha, they began crossing the Himalayas with what was developing into a very popular religious teaching. As early as 54 C.E. a community was living in China under royal patronage and the Chinese had begun to build monasteries where disciples recited Buddhist sutras, copied manuscripts into Chinese, and evoked a passion for the new religion from India. As it merged with prevalent beliefs, China's own particular form of Buddhism emerged.

Bodhidharma Brings Zen to China

At about the same time that Buddha appeared in India, Lao Tzu had appeared in China. By the time Bodhidharma arrived both Taoism and Buddhism were prevalent, as were a host of lesser-known traditions. The spiritual climate in China had greatly degraded and people worshiped in a half-hearted way, believing that empty-hearted prayers and donations of food or money would serve at least as well as devotion to influence their future. Religion had become an affair of show and had little to do with the sincere desire to discover the truths of human nature.

It was into this climate that Bodhidharma arrived. He was a strange man, powerful in appearance and uncompromising in the truths that he spoke. Word began to spread that a "real" Buddha had arrived in China and people flocked to see him, but Bodhidharma was not so available as they supposed. Arriving at his meeting place, those who wanted to talk and ask him questions were met by his backside. Bodhidharma sat facing a wall, saying nothing. People would leave in a huff and others would arrive. No one stayed for long, and all were puzzled by his powerful presence—and a little bit afraid.

Bodhidharma would not move. He simply sat in silence, staring at the wall. This silence, although interrupted by those who tried to get him to turn around and answer questions, was undisturbed for nine years. Bodhidharma, it was rumored, was waiting for someone to come who deserved his attention. This man finally came in the person of Hui K'o. After sitting silently for some time, Hui K'o cut off his hand and threw it at Bodhidharma. The master turned around.

After the arrival of Hui K'o, a small group of seekers followed Bodhidharma into the countryside where they lived in caves, for a profound displeasure with the unrefined ways of this new sort of Buddhism was beginning to show itself.

Bodhidharma's approach was a radical departure from traditional ways of Chinese decorum and Buddhist piety. He did not visit temples. He did not recite sutras. Instead he was gruff and unpretentious. He had his disciples sit and stare at an empty wall, and then, with loud noises and sudden shocks he provoked them into immediate experiences of what he called no-mind. His methods were simple and direct—and his disciples very few.

Before Bodhidharma's death he passed his work on to Hui K'o. Taking off his yellow robe, Bodhidharma said, "Just as Buddha handed a flower to Mahakashyapa, so I am giving to you my yellow robe. Use it when trust is slight and doubts arise. People will say that Buddha is a man of India and you, Hui K'o, are a man of China, and they will ask you to prove the transmission that has been passed on to you. This robe will act as a sign."

After the death of Bodhidharma, Hui K'o and his disciples continued the practice of silently gazing at an empty wall. As they moved slowly about the country they continued to provoke each other with intuitive insights and surprise actions. A new lightheartedness entered their world. They ceased to be bogged down by complicated interpretations of Buddha's teachings and found a simplicity that grew in its appeal and which slowly began to be practiced in China. This new teaching was called Ch'an. Many years later, when it was carried to Japan, it was called Zen. The word Ch'an is derived from the Sanskrit word *dhyan* which means "meditation."

Bodhidharma later become known as the First Patriarch of Zen. Hui K'o was the Second Patriarch and his disciple Sosan was the third. Sosan was a gentle, friendly man who followed Hui K'o from mountain cave to mountain cave fleeing the persecution of the Chinese. After his own enlightenment, Sosan, fearing that the Zen teachings of Bodhidharma would be lost to the world, wrote a short poem called *Hsinhsinming*, which was very a concise description of this new way. The *Hsinhsinming* of Sosan is one of the most inspiring, precise, and insightful glimpses into any description of Zen. The Chinese characters that make up the title are three individual pictures. One shows trust, one shows heart, and one shows soul.

Words!

Zen is beyond language,

for in it there is

no yesterday

no tomorrow

no today.

Zen is not difficult

for those who have no preferences.

When love and hate are both absent

everything becomes clear and undisguised.

Make the smallest distinction, however,

and heaven and earth are set infinitely apart.

If you wish to see the truth

then hold no opinions for or against anything.

The struggle with what one likes and what one dislikes

is the disease of the mind.

SOSAN

To live in Zen is to live in meditation and to be constantly aware of the nature of mind. The continual preferences of for and against, this and that, yesterday and tomorrow are simply a disease of the mind. The practice of Zen is to recognize the disease, catch hold of it, and let it go.

Sosan's successor was Hyakujo. Before him, Hui K'o and Sosan had been wanderers, traveling mostly in hiding, nurturing this new way. Neither of them had many disciples, but those they had were devoted.

Hyakujo founded the first Zen community. Drawing more than five hundred disciples, he found himself in a situation that was forever to alter the face of

Buddhism. Until this time, Buddhist monks had always been supported either by members of a community that gave food to the begging monks, or by the rich who donated land for them to stay on. Benefactors and royalty maintained large monasteries that supported the translation of Buddhist texts.

But Zen had not found the support that was needed for five hundred disciples, all wanting to practice meditation. Begging certainly could not support them all. So, in response to this situation, Hyakujo set up a small monastery in which the monks themselves shared in the task of supporting their lifestyle.

"A day without work is a day without food," he said, and the Zen community devised creative ways to support itself, and, thus existed independently of outside influences. No longer wandering beggars, Zen monks established a new tradition of their own. Whether chopping wood or carrying water from the well, the disciples of Zen would concentrate on sensing into the present moment. Enlightenment ceased to be the final awakening that was realized after years of hard work. It became a sudden realization, a flowering that could occur in a moment.

These words from Bodhidharma give further insight into Zen.

To find a Buddha all you have to do is see your nature. Your nature is the Buddha. And the Buddha is the person who's free—free of plans, free of cares.

If you don't see your nature and run around all day looking somewhere else, you'll never find a Buddha.

The truth is, there's nothing to find. But to reach such an understanding you need a teacher and you need to struggle to make yourself understand. Life and death are important. Don't suffer them in vain. There's no advantage in deceiving yourself. Even if you have mountains of jewels and as many servants as there are grains of sand along the Ganges, you see them when your eyes are open. But what about when your eyes are shut? You should realize then that everything you see is like a dream or illusion.

If you don't find a teacher soon, you'll live this life in vain. It's true, you have the Buddha-nature. But without the help of a teacher you'll never know it. Only one person in a million becomes enlightened without a teacher's help.

In the years of the early Zen monks in China there was a new mingling of the truths which were handed down from Buddha and those which came from Lao Tzu. This meeting of Buddhism and Taoism was a unique moment in history: Two religious traditions met and did not erupt in violence, but coexisted peacefully.

Out of Bodhidharma's methods the new teaching called Ch'an, or Zen, became very popular. Wandering monks came from Japan and Korea to study with the Chinese mystics. What they took back to their countries was the small bud of a flower that was eventually to wander across oceans to lands that were as yet unknown.

Not thinking about anything is Zen.

Once you know this, walking, standing, sitting or lying down,

everything you do is Zen.

To know that the mind is empty is to see the Buddha.

BODHIDHARMA

Zen Arrives in Japan

Buddhism was officially introduced to Japan in 522 C.E. when a Korean king sent a request for military aid. His messengers brought with them as a gift an image of the Buddha and a scroll of scriptures. They promised that anyone converting to Buddhism would have good fortune, and the Japanese emperor believed them. The new religion caught on like wildfire especially among the elite—and mostly because it was believed to possess a greater magic than that found in other rituals.

Kakua was one of the first Japanese monks to travel to China to study, and while he was there he attained enlightenment. He did not travel much but lived on a mountain in a remote part of the country where he meditated constantly. Whenever people found him and asked him to preach, he would say a few words, and then he would move to another part of the mountain where he could be found less easily.

Eventually Kakua returned home. The emperor of Japan heard about him and ordered him to come to the court to speak about Zen. Kakua went before the emperor and stood for a while in silence. He then produced a flute from the folds of his robes, blew one short note, bowed politely, and disappeared. No one ever knew what became of Kakua.

During its earliest period Buddhism was tremendously popular in Japan and many different schools flourished; but by the 12th century it had suffered a severe deterioration due partly to the fact that Japan was so cut off from the rest of the Buddhist world.

Meanwhile, in China, Buddhist monasteries had also grown decadent, sometimes providing little more than entertainment for local rulers. The Ch'an School of Bodhidharma was the only one that kept the real spirit of Buddhism alive.

A number of monks in Japan grew concerned about the laxity and they sought to bring about reforms. The most popular of these was Eisai, who breathed the new life of Zen into Buddhism.

At the age of eleven he entered the local temple as a monk. Having quickly become convinced that something was missing, he set his heart on going to

China where he hoped to receive a purer teaching. While he was waiting for the opportunity to sail west, he met a Chinese interpreter who told him about the emergence of Bodhidharma's Ch'an school. Although its methods seemed strange, Eisai was inspired to seek out this group for he sensed that its teachings might offer him what he was looking for.

At the age of twenty-seven he sailed to China where he met another young monk with whom he visited several monasteries that taught Ch'an. When he returned to Japan, he brought sixty volumes of scriptures with him, depositing them in a temple library. Realizing the subtlety of the practices he had learned, Eisai refrained from instructing others in what he had picked up, and immersed himself in his own personal studies. Meanwhile he prepared for a more extensive journey back to China. It was during this second trip that he met and studied with Rinzai, and became enlightened himself.

Some years later Eisai returned to Japan and established the school of Rinzai Zen. At this time he is reported to have also brought tea from China, advocating it as an aid to meditation. It is said by some that Bodhidharma had once cut his eyelashes and sown them in the ground, producing the plant that would keep those who practiced meditation from nodding off.

In the thirteenth century, a Japanese monk named Dogen founded a second school of Zen known as Soto. As a novice he had become completely puzzled by the question: If all living beings have Buddha-nature, then why do monks engage in practice? Seeking an answer, he eventually found his way to China where he trained under two great masters. He returned to Japan a few years later and taught a simple sitting meditation. So many disciples flocked to learn from him that he had to move several times to larger temples.

Both Rinzai and Soto Zen teach a simple sitting meditation called zazen. Both have the same purpose, which is known in Japanese as *satori*. Satori is the Japanese word that means "to know" and refers to the wisdom that comes with enlightenment.

Koans

The purpose of the sitting meditation that is taught in Zen is to still the mind. Soto Zen adds to this the practice of responding to a koan—a type of meditation upon a paradox. The concept of the koan originated in China during the time of Bodhidharma. The wild antics that marked the study of Ch'an were the early attempts to find ways to shock students into an awareness of the present moment. Perhaps the most well-known koan is, "What is the sound of one hand clapping?"

A koan cannot be solved with reason. In searching for an appropriate response a disciple grapples with an attempt to say something that is totally spontaneous. The only way to do this is to be one hundred percent in the present moment.

The koans and the stories of the antics that developed as they were responded to, have become a popular method of describing the very essence of Zen. Sometimes difficult to understand, they all carry a high sense of lightheartedness, and although they may seem to be irrational they give great insight into the wily wisdom of Zen—a wisdom that exists only in the here and now.

A newcomer asked to be shown the way to the monastery and Chao-chou replied,
"Have you finished eating your rice?"

———

The monks of the eastern and western halls were arguing about a cat. Nan-ch'uan
came by, picked up the cat and said, "If you can say the right word, I'll spare the cat.
If not, I'll kill it." Nobody spoke. Nan-ch'uan killed the cat.

———

Later, Chao-chou returned to the monastery. He entered Nan-ch'uan's room.
Nan-ch'uan told him what happened. Without a word, Chao-chou took off his
sandals, put them on his head, turned around and walked out of the room.
As he was leaving Nan-ch'uan said, "If only you had been here,
I would not have killed the cat."

In later years there was a master named Dogo who had a disciple called Soshin. When Soshin was taken in as a novice, he expected to be taught Zen the way a schoolboy is taught at school. But Dogo gave no special lessons on the subject. This bewildered and disappointed Soshin.

One day he said to the master, "It is some time since I came here, but not a word has been given to me regarding the essence of the Zen teaching."

Dogo replied, "Since your arrival I have been giving you lessons every moment on the matter of Zen discipline."

"What kind of lesson could that have been?" the novice wondered.

"When you bring me a cup of tea in the morning, I take it; when you serve me a meal, I accept it; when you bow to me, I return it with a nod. How else do you expect to be taught the discipline of Zen?"

Soshin hung his head for a while, pondering the puzzling words of the master. Dogo said, "If you want to see, see at once. When you begin to think, you miss the point."

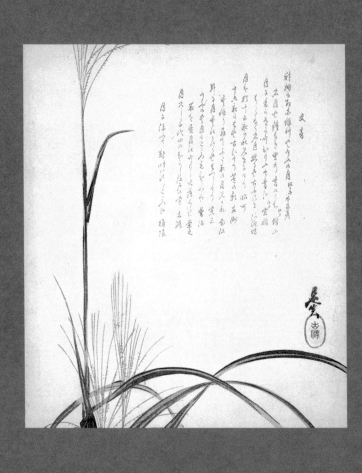

Haiku

Over the last several hundred years, Zen has became inextricably woven into the heart and mind of Japanese culture. Matsuo Basho brought the insights of Zen into the public arena through his poetry—creating a form that is known to us as haiku.

A haiku is a poem that can be said in a single breath and which conveys an experience of a particular moment. Those verses that succeed have arisen spontaneously just as do the responses to a koan. Like koans, the practice of writing haiku has become a trademark of Zen.

In the summer of 1684, Basho started out on a long walking journey during which he kept a journal called *The Records of a Weather-Exposed Skeleton*. In this famous book he recounts the making of his poetry. He begins by saying:

Following the example of the ancient priest who is said to have traveled thousands of miles caring naught for his provisions and attaining the state of sheer ecstasy under the pure beams of the moon, I left my house on the River Sumida among the wails of the Autumn wind.

Like the sound of a fire crackling:
River snow,
Melting.

KEIKO ITO

A red sun
Falls into the sea:
What summer heat!

NATSUME SOSEKI

Fallen leaves—
Raking,
Yet not raking.

TAIGI

Come, let's go
Snow-viewing
Till we're buried.

BASHO

Ten Bulls of Zen

In the twelfth century the Chinese Zen master Kakuan drew ten pictures that have become famous as the Ten Bulls of Zen. These pictures have been reproduced and redrawn time and time again, for they depict, more beautifully than words, the story of those who seek to know themselves through Zen. They describe the seeker who embarks upon a journey to discover the true essence of his being.

Seeking to discover the bull, carrying the staff of purpose and the wine jug of true desire, a young boy sets out. He discovers the footprints and follows them until he reaches the bull who he tames. He then returns to the world with the bull on the end of a rope.

A final picture shows no boy and no bull, for seeker and sought have dissolved and only the present moment remains. This present moment is the source of Zen's wisdom. It is a wisdom that words cannot satisfactorily convey; but the art, the poetry and the antics of Zen masters give us a feeling and a taste for the true and joyful spontaneity that is Zen.

SUMMARY

The saints and mystics of Eastern wisdom are men and women who, like ourselves, were born into this world. Their everyday experiences indicated that there is more to life than meets the eye, and so they embarked upon a quest of discovery.

The words of the Eastern mystics, the ways that they lived, their poetry and art, and the stories they told, all this contributes to an experience and a wisdom that enriches our inner world. Sufis convey to us the understanding that God lies within the human heart. Taoist wisdom tells us that we are cared for by the same energetic phenomena that watches over the movements of the sun and the stars. Zen points clearly to a paradise that is here and now.

It has long been recognized by all those who become acquainted with Eastern wisdom that the greatest acts of love and compassion are the words and deeds of the mystics, saints and sages, for they have journeyed within, they have traversed the whole inner landscape and they truly know who they are. It is said in the East that the only real road to peace lies within ourselves. Life's greatest adventure begins when we begin to walk down that path.

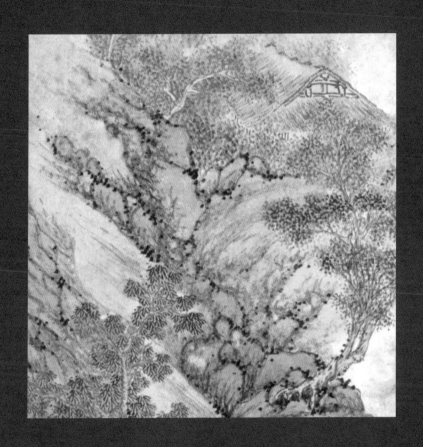

ACKNOWLEDGEMENTS

Cover: Spring Dawn at the Elixir Terrace; National Palace Museum, Taiwan.

Page 4: Autumn Moon Over the Dew Terrace; Museum für Ostasiatische Kunst, Cologne.

Page 7: Two Dervishes Meditating; British Museum, London.

Page 8: Bridge Over Mountain Stream by Fan K'uan; British Museum, London.

Page 10: Dancing Dervishes; British Museum, London.

Page 12: Miniature of Sufi Poet, Yunus Emre; Roland and Sabrina Michaud.

Page 14: Pilgrims at the Ka'bah; Chester Beatty Library, Dublin.

Page 17: British Library, London.

Page 18: The Prophet Muhammed; Turkish & Islamic Art Museum, Istanbul.

Page 21: The Ascension of the Prophet Muhammed; The British Library, London.

Page 22: Two Physicians; Werner Forman Archives, London.

Page 24: Riyad Plays and Sings to the Lady; Biblioteca Apostolica Vaticana, Rome.

Page 26: Youth Reading; British Museum, London.

Page 29: Prince Being Entertained in the Countryside; British Museum, London.

Page 31: Girl Writing; British Library, London.

Page 34: Portrait of an Aged Mullah; Ancient Art & Architecture Collection, London.

Page 37: A King Becomes a Hermit's Disciple; Freer Gallery of Art, Washington, D.C.

Page 39: The Poet Sadi in Ecstasy; The al-Sabah Collection, Kuwait.

Page 40: Court Scene; Victoria & Albert Museum, London.

Page 43: Abu Zayd With a Man Who Speaks in Verse; Bibliothèque Nationale de France, Paris.

Page 44: Portrait of Rumi; British Museum, London.

ACKNOWLEDGEMENTS

Page 46: Musicians; British Library, London.

Page 48: Dervish Holding Leaf; Victoria & Albert Museum, London.

Page 50: Abu Zayd and Harith; Bodleian Library, Oxford.

Page 52: Scene From the Khamsah of Amir Khusrau; Chester Beatty Library, Dublin.

Page 56: The 'Jade Lady' Among the Clouds; Gulbenkian Museum, Durham.

Page 59: The Immortal Li Tieguai; Chion-ji, Kyoto.

Page 60: Diagram of the Supreme Ultimate; University of Chicago Library, Chicago.

Page 63: The Old Man of the Southern Pole; Palace Museum, Beijing

Page 64: Procession of the Gods of the Heavenly Constellations; Gulbenkian Museum, Durham.

Page 67: Gathering of Immortals at Yaochi; Asian Art Museum, San Francisco.

Page 68: Portrait of Lao Tzu by Qian Gu; British Museum, London.

Page 71: Lao Tzu on an Ox by Zhang Lu; National Palace Museum, Taiwan.

Page 73: Autumn Moon Over the Dew Terrace; Museum für Ostasiatische Kunst, Cologne.

Page 74: British Museum, London.

Page 77: Wind in Pines Among a Myriad Valleys by Li Tang; National Palace Museum, Taiwan.

Page 78: A Chinese Sage Admiring a Waterfall; Christie's Images, New York.

Page 81: Tiger and Magpie; Cultural Service, Korean Embassy, Tokyo.

Page 84: Chuang Tzu Dreaming of a Butterfly; Palace Museum, Beijing.

Page 87: Taking a Qin to Visit a Friend by Jiang Song; British Museum, London.

Page 88: Poet Reading by a Stream; British Museum, London.

Page 91: Boating by Moonlight; British Museum, London.

Page 92: National Gallery, Prague.

Page 95: Dragonfly; British Museum, London.

Page 96: Pavilions on a Mountainside; National Palace Museum, Taiwan.

Page 98: Album of Landscapes and Figures by Jin Nong; Shanghai Museum, Shanghai.

Page 100: British Museum, London.

Page 103: Buddha with Five Tathagatas: Metropolitan Museum of Art, New York.

Page 104: Butterfly and Reed; Peking Museum, Peking.

Page 107: Ajanta cave frescos Bodhisattvas; © Philip Baud.

Page 108: British Museum, London.

Page 111: Book Cover with Scenes from the Life of Buddha; Private Collection.

Page 112: Self Portrait by Hakuin; Eisei Bunko Foundation, Tokyo.

Page 115: Reading in the Autumn; Peking Museum, Peking.

Page 116: Daruma; Private Collection.

Page 118: Boy on a Buffalo; Freer Gallery of Art, Washington, D.C.

Page 121: Man with Umbrella; British Museum, London.

Page 122: Flowering Pear Tree; Peking Museum, Peking.

Page 124: In the Spirit of Poems by Du Fu; Shanghai Museum, Shanghai.

Page 127: Looking Toward the Waterfall; Gulbenkian Museum, Durham.

Page 129: Album of Landscapes and Figures by Jin Nong; Shanghai Museum, Shanghai.

Page 130: Li Po; Freer Gallery of Art, Washington, D.C.

Page 133: Daruma; Collection of J.E.V.M. Kingado, USA.

Page 135: British Museum, London.

Page 136: Bodhidharma in Meditation by Hakuin; Eisei Bunko Foundation, Tokyo.

Page 139: Zen Parable; Collection of J.E.V.M. Kingado, USA.

Pages 141, 142: British Museum, London.

Page 145: Hotei: Collection of J.E.V.M. Kingado, USA.